Jihad Shmihad,
What Were You Thinking?!

By S. R. Morris

Table of Contents

Jihad Shmihad,
What Were You Thinking??!!

Anger Management is a 2003 American movie starring Adam Sandler and Jack Nicholson. In the film, Sandler loses his temper during an airline flight and, after being tased by airline marshals, he is sentenced to enroll in anger management classes designed to help him get his temper under control.

Once again, radical Muslims have dominated the news here in the U.S. and around the world. Some have legitimately asked why Muslims are so angry about little things that most of the civilized world would ignore or just express (verbally) their disgust.

Why do Muslims take everything so personally (like everything revolves around them), and why do they fly off the handle so quickly? Why do they always respond with violence? Haven't they ever heard of anger management?

Recently, I read an article published by the Mayo Clinic that effectively addresses this topic in a meaningful way. In the interest of bringing peace to everyone involved, I have adopted some tips that may help followers of Mohammad (the angriest man on the planet—EVER) deal with their feelings of insecurity and control their tempers.

8 Anger Management Tips for 'Moderate' Muslims

Do you fume when you hear someone who said something, that someone else told someone else, who told you that Mohammad was a pedophile? Does your blood pressure rocket when you hear that someone is drawing a cartoon that makes fun of your prophet?

While anger is a normal and even healthy emotion — it's important to deal with it in a positive way, and not rape, burn and behead someone. Uncontrolled anger can take a toll on both your health (like a drone) and everyone around you.

Are you ready to get your anger under control? You can start by implementing these 8 anger management tips in your life.

1) Think before you cut someone's head off (literally)

In the heat of the moment, when you see a cartoon of Mohammad looking like a rabid dog frothing at the mouth and swinging a sword like a madman, it's easy to do the same and look like a complete idiot. Take a minute to collect your thoughts before you do something only a headhunter from Borneo would do. Don't be swept away by feelings of insecurity and count to 10 (or 10,000 if necessary) until you regain control of your temper.

2) Once you're calm, express your anger in a peaceful way

In a few years, when you're thinking clearly, express your frustration in a positive way. Don't be confrontational. State your concerns and frustrations (about Mohammad, the Quran, your inability to get and keep a girlfriend, etc.) and do so without hurting others or trying to control them.

3) Take a timeout

Timeouts aren't just for kids or infidels. Give yourself short breaks during times of the day that tend to be stressful, such as your inability to convince others that Islam is a religion of peace. A few moments (hours, days, or weeks depending on your insecurity) of quiet time might help you feel better about yourself without getting so angry you want to place the paperboy in a cage and light his backpack on fire.

4) Identify possible solutions

Instead of focusing on what made you mad, take a lesson on basket weaving, origami or a class on comparative religions. Does it drive you crazy when the checker at the grocery store scans packages of ham or bacon without cursing the infidels in the line? Take a breath. Move to another checkout line (not the one that accepts liquor purchases). Remind yourself that chopping off the hands of fellow customers won't fix anything and will only make everything bloody.

5) Stick with 'I' statements

Avoid criticizing or placing blame. Use "I" statements to describe the problem. Be respectful and specific. For example, say, "I'm upset that you doodled a figure that may be understood by others as a caricature of Mohammad, who was the perfect man and wrote the perfect book Quran and gave us the peaceful religion of Islam."

6) Don't hold a grudge by living in the past

Try to forget and forgive how several Muslim countries got their butts kicked by a few Israelis in the 6 Day War in 1967. Try to forget and forgive that Sadam Hussein lost twice to the U.S. and ended up living in a hole in the ground like a rat. Forgiveness is a powerful tool and can be liberating. If you allow anger and other negative feelings to take control, you might find yourself swallowed up by your own bitterness or sense of injustice. It's unrealistic to expect everyone in the civilized world to behave like barbarians.

7) Practice relaxation skills

When your temper flares, put relaxation skills to work. Imagine a relaxing scene, like receiving your allocation of 72 virgins when you . . . (no, scratch that one). Try repeat a calming word or phrase, such as "Allahu Akbar" . . . (no, scratch that one too). Try listening to music or write in a journal or draw a picture of . . . (no, scratch that last one too).

8) Get professional help

Learning to control your anger can be a real challenge, especially when you still live in medieval times. Seek help. If you can't find peace of mind in a peaceful religion, consider changing religions.

Remember: everything doesn't revolve around you and a double-edged sword. Try to find some peace in your own mind before you try to sever someone else's. Take it from Barack Hussein Obama, a master at masking his anger and religion, "Stop clinging to your religion and your swords" and join the 21st century.

4 Summer Sex Tips
When You're Wearing a Burka

Recently, *Huffington Post* published an article titled "5 Sizzling Summer Sex Tips." Since I'm a follower of fashion trends, I decided to investigate and see if they had any "tips" for women who were relegated to wearing a burka.

Although *Huff Po* lists 5 tips for women living in the West, I could not find any that would help the well-dressed burka woman. As a result, I decided to write my own tips for the burka crowd (and you can see by the photo above, there is a real crowd interested in my tips).

1) Take a fantasy vacation.

Summer is a hot time so weather is a real concern while wearing a burka. But who says you can't sizzle and be sexy? (Disregard this advice if your husband is a member of ISIS or your imam is a real stick in the mud fundamentalist.)

Make your own tropical lubricant using olive oil. Apply the oil liberally to your body before slipping into your husband's favorite burka. Then, walk around the kitchen as if nothing is different. In no time the aroma of your body will arrest the attention of your horny hubby and he will whisk you away from the kitchen and hump you faster than a camel with two humps. (For a faster response, use extra virgin oil, and you may not even leave the kitchen!)

2) Don't forget the drought!

Depending on which Middle Eastern country you call home (or prison), there is probably a drought, or shortage of water. Remember, your body has its own cooling method and it's called sweating. If it's been a long time since you showered, try to collect as much of hubby's sweat and, for a longer shower or sponge bath, apply it to your own (sweat is basically moisture). Don't rinse off too quickly. If you make lots of noise (and your husband allows it) and he may even want seconds.

3) Go sightseeing!

While uncovering parts of your body is prohibited except when you're alone with your loving soul mate (or soul master as the case may be), sex is the ideal time to begin doing some sightseeing on your vacation.

If he prefers that you spend a lot of time on your back, it may be the perfect time to examine the ceiling to determine whether it needs a new coat of paint. If he prefers "sheepie style" methods, the best you can hope for is a "dream" vacation (yes, short naps are allowed).

4) Pretend you're at the beach.

It's not too hard to imagine that! A great imaginary beach vacation can be achieved by making the proper preparations. First, get a blanket and place it on ground. After that, your mind has no limits. Get creative. A suggestion is to take a handful of sand and place it near the blanket. Your vacation at the beach is almost complete. Make sure you are near a window where the sun is brightly illuminating the room.

Summer is a hot time, but being confined to a Muslim country surrounded by fanatics, and wearing a burka, doesn't mean you can't have fun. Make your own fun and create your own dream vacation. The solution is all in your mind.

The Islamic State Newlywed Game

(We join this program which is already underway.)

HOST: Okay, we've taken your husbands off stage so they can't hear your responses to the following questions: What is your husband's favorite color?

Aaeesha: Black

Aarzoo: Black

Durriya: Black

Baharbano: Sometimes he likes me to wear an olive drab color, sometimes white if I put a lot of virgin olive oil in his dinner, but mostly black.

HOST: Okay, but we can only record one answer. So what do you think he will say?

Baharbano: Black

HOST: Okay. Second set of questions. How many dates did you have before you got married?

Aaeesha: I ate a whole handful because I love dates. But I know you're looking for a number, so I would say 12.

Aarzoo: I love dates too, so I would say 10.

Durriya: I'm going to say 7.

Baharbano: I'm going to have to say 72 because I've got a real sweet tooth and I counted them so I could make a good impression on my husband.

HOST: I'm not sure you understood my question, but let's just move on. Which type of vehicle best describes your husband's sex drive?

Aaeesha: My husband is like a standard sedan, but he does prefer a car with rear drive transmission.

Aarzoo: My husband is like a 4WD truck with all four wheels always in motion, if you know what I mean.

Durriya: My husband is a convertible. He always likes to drive with the top down.

Baharbano: I want to say he's like an ATV (All Terrain Vehicle) because he doesn't care where it happens or how dirty things get.

HOST: Okay ladies. Final question for this round before I bring the husbands back to ask them questions. What TV show best describes your husband?

Aaeesha: That's a hard question. My first thought was *"All in the Family"* because he's married two of his cousins too, but I'd have to say *"The Honeymooners."* We've been married 12 years, but everyone time I complain that I have a headache, he says. "Hey, we're still honeymooners."

Aarzoo: I'm like Aaeesha; I had two thoughts. The first thing I thought of was *"Saturday Night Live"* because it's as regular as clockwork in our tent. But I'm going to have to go with *"60 Minutes"* because sometimes it's hard to stay awake.

Durriya: That's easy. *"Sex in the City"* because every time we go into city . . . well. It's definitely *"Sex in the City."*

Baharbano: My answer has to be **"Buffy the Vampire Slayer."** Mohammad really gets excited whenever he sees a sword. He's a real jihadist fanatic because whenever he even hears about a beheading he will—

HOST: Okay ladies. Thanks for sharing your answers. After this short commercial break, we're going to bring your husbands in and ask them some questions.

BREAK

HOST: For our viewers at home, I want to explain that we had to assign different names for the husbands since they are all named Mohammad. We chose to use their second name instead, except in the case of Mohammad Muhammad, we have used his first name—Mohammad.
Okay gentlemen. Here are your questions: What color are your wife's eyes?

Abdul: Black, I think.

Faarooq: I'm not sure, but I think they're black. Yeah, I'm going to say black.

Zaabit: Black. No, brown. No, green, yes they must be green, but . . . no, I'm going to go with my first choice, black.

Mohammad: I haven't looked for a long time, but they better be blue.

HOST: Second question gentlemen. When your wife was 13, what did she want to be when she grew up?

Abdul: We already have two children, so I'm sure she wants to have at least 5 more and I'm going to say a mother.

Faarooq: I'm not sure. I remember at 11 she wanted more children, so I'm going to say mother too.

Zaabit: She was 12 when we married so I'm sure that she wanted to be my wife when she was 13. I'm going to say wife.

Mohammad: My wife always wanted to be a jihadist bride, and her dream came true when she married me.

HOST: Next question. Which of your wife's best friends look best in a burka?

Abdul: Durriya. That's her little sister. I've often imagined her in a burka in my tent.

Faarooq: Haalimah. That's my brother's daughter. She's always swishing around in an olive drab burka and it just drives me wild.

Zaabit: Obaidiyah. She one of my wife's friend and she herds goats. I'd have to say Obaidiyah, but I fantasize her in a burka riding my favorite goat.

Mohammad: Elma. She's the daughter of my uncle's second wife. She'd be a knockout in a white burka.

HOST: Last question. If allied forces were attacking your town, and you had only a few minutes before the attack, what 3 things would you save?

Abdul: My knife, my sword and my camel.

HOST: Abdul, you wouldn't take your wife?

Abdul: Jihadi wives are a dime a dozen at the slave market. You asked what 3 things I would take and that's my answer.

Faarooq: My sword, a sheep's intestine full of hummus, and my favorite goat.

Zaabit: My sword, my AK 47, and an RPG (rocket propelled grenade).

Mohammad: That's easy. My sword, a jar of olive oil, and any camel or goat I could find.

HOST: We'll be right back after the commercial break and see what the wives have to say. In case of a tie, we asked both wives and husbands a tie breaker. For the husbands we asked "What's your wife's burka size?" and for the wives we've asked, "What is the breed of your husband's favorite goat?"

Stay tuned for more

Beekeepers or Burka Models?

(My apologies to apiarists. Please do not be offended of this post, unless you are Muslim. Go ahead and be offended because I know you will anyway.)

ISIS Announces Woman of the Year

An anonymous spokesman for the Islamic State announced today that Zubeidat Tsarnaeva, mother of the Boston Marathon bomber, has been voted the Mother of the Year. Voting came after delegates from all the caliphates recognized in various parts of the world chose her for the title.

"She spoke for all Islamic jihadists everywhere," the IS official said. "That's why she was chosen to be the IS Woman of the Year."

"They will pay for my sons and the sons of Islam, permanently!!!" the mother from hell threatened America. "The tears of their mothers will be fuel for them in hell."

Her "best son" Dzhokar was found guilty of all 30 charges related to the bombing. He was sentenced to the death penalty and the "Mother of the Year" lamented it before the world.

Despite that fact that Dzhokar and her "second best" son were responsible for killing three people (including an 8-year-old boy) and injuring 260 (17 of which lost limbs in the bombing), she had praises for her "precious" son.

They were "glorious and rare in character and essence," says bomber mommy, and added they are "the best sons of their mother and also the best sons of their religion."

While others believe she spawned demons, officials of the Islamic State believe she is a model of Islamic womanhood. What do you think?

It's a Thing Called 'Intelligence'

I dislike spreading rumors, but this story has been verified by many of my sources (although they wish to remain anonymous). Warning: Be careful sharing this story with Muslims (or liberals), who have no sense of humor.

This story is about two factory workers somewhere in the Middle East. They were not too happy when a new young employee got a raise and a promotion. During a break, the two older fellows began discussing why the new employee got a promotion.

Abdul: I don't think it's fair that he got a raise and a promotion.

Muhammad: Yeah. It's not fair. You've worked here for over 5 years. I've worked here for almost 10 years and I've never had a raise or a promotion. Why go you think he got a promotion?

Abdul: I don't know. Why don't you just go to the boss and ask him?

During their lunch break, Muhammad went to see the boss and asked.

Muhammad: Some of us were just wondering why we never get raises and we've been working here for years. This new guy has only been here a few months and he got a raise and a promotion. Why is that?

Farooq the Boss: That's simple. It's called intelligence.

Muhammad: Intelligence? What's that?

Farooq the Boss: Here. Let me show you.

Farooq the Boss got up from his desk and walked up to a steel beam in the doorway of his office. He placed his open hand on the beam and turned to the worker.

Farooq the Boss: Okay. Now just make a fist and hit my hand as hard as you can.

Muhammad: I can't do that boss! I could hurt you.

Farooq the Boss: No, that's okay. I want you to hit my hand as hard as you can, and I won't hold it against you.

Muhammad: Okay, if you say so.

Muhammad made a fist, wound up, and unleashed a powerful punch. But just a fraction of a second before Muhammad delivered the punch, Farooq the Boss pulled his hand away from the steel post. Muhammad's fist hit the beam and it resulted in excruciating pain for Muhammad.

Farooq the Boss: Now, that's intelligence.

Later, when Muhammad returned to the factory floor, Abdul asked him the obvious question.

Abdul: Well, did you find out why the boss gave the new guy a raise and we didn't get one?

Muhammad: Yeah. It's called intelligence.

Abdul: Intelligence? What's that?

Smiling, Muhammad took his open hand and placed it in front of his own face.

Muhammad: Just hit my hand as hard as you can.

What's the Difference?

Here's a question for all defenders of Islam. What's the difference between headhunting among tribes like the Dayak in Borneo or the Nagas in Indonesia and beheading people in the name of Islam?

Defenders of Islam would say that Islam is a religion and the only reason for beheading a person is because the offender broke Islam's laws. But that's not true.

Many headhunting tribes believe that the head represents the core personality of an enemy and to take their head is not only an act of violence that puts fear in an enemy's heart but also serves as an insult to the victim and his family. Isn't that what followers of Islam believe also?

In some headhunting societies, beheading an enemy is considered a rite of manhood and young men may marry a wife until they have taken a head in battle. Isn't that what Islamic terrorists believe when they "award" a jihadi wife after they have proved themselves in battle against the enemies of Allah?

Victorious headhunters display the heads of their enemies as trophies. Beheading an enemy increases the reputation of the tribe and intimidates current and future enemies. Isn't that what the Islamic State and all its subsidiaries (ISIS, ISIL, etc.) do to infidels who do not acknowledge Mohammad as the great prophet of Islam?

But Islam is a religion that people respect, so their barbaric practices should be allowed, right?

Part of Borneo is inhabited by the Dayak, a variety of indigenous native tribes, who believe that everything living - animal, vegetable, or human - is endowed with a spiritual identity. One of the souls of a person is believed to reside in the head and by taking someone else's head, it is pleasing in the eyes of their gods. Have you heard a similar excuse from the followers of Mohammad?

The practices of primitive tribes of headhunting are now frowned upon by government authorities and religious organizations. Why aren't more governments and religious organizations speaking out against these barbaric acts by Islamic tribes or radical followers of Mohammad?

What about the Nagas?

Located in the mountains of northeastern India, the Nagas practice headhunting. They say it is an important practice because it ensures the success of their crops and depended on the sprinkling of a stranger's blood over the fields. With the influence of Christianity the barbaric customs of the Nagas have changed. Now most Nagas take the heads of monkeys (instead of humans) and display them on baskets

Aren't followers of Mohammad and radical Islam able to forsake savage customs and live peacefully with the rest of the civilized world? Isn't it time that leaders of Muslim countries (including our own POTUS) tell them to stop clinging to their barbaric religious customs and their arms (knives, swords, etc.) and join the 21st century?

Breaking News from ISIS

Breaking News!

This just out of Syria: Our ME (Middle Eastern) reporter states that ISIS has a new strain of ISIS that is now calling itself the Reformed Islamic State of Quran Ultimate Exposed (RISQUE). The splinter group has taken over a portion of Syria and Iraq that had previously belonged exclusively to ISIS.

According to reports, RISQUE has been dissatisfied with the quantity and quality of jihadi brides imported for their fighters. Leaders of the new group has been working behind the scenes to bring more Muslim women into the area who keep the fighters happy on their days off.

Our ME reporter secretly interviewed one of the RISQUE leaders to find out if there was any truth of the rumors. Video and audio of the interview could not be smuggled out of the area, but an English transcript of the interview has been reviewed and we are now making it available to our readers.

MEP (Middle Eastern Reporter): We have been hearing some rumors about your group and your dissatisfaction with the rest of ISIS. Can you give me more details?

Abdul X (Name is changed so he can keep his head): Yes. It's true. RISQUE has broken away from ISIS because we are more liberal and we want to keep our fighters happy.

MEP: We've heard similar reports of groups who have promised a new camel or goat to keep fighters happy.

Abdul X: It's true because the promise of jihadi brides has been drying up. Many of the new brides are in their 50s and 60s and can barely walk without assistance. To avoid a mutiny, some groups have brought in whole herds of camels and goats. But we've taken a whole new approach.

MEP: What are you doing that's different?

Abdul X: We've purchased a group of very beautiful women, but we don't give them to the fighters. Instead, we invite them to come to one of our clubs and they are welcome to view the women as they partially disrobe.

MEP: What??!! You mean you have actually opened a strip joint for your fighters right here in Syria?

Abdul X: Yes. The women begin dancing in front of the fighters and the men are encouraged to throw money at the feet of the women as they dance. They move around and dance to the music as they begin to remove some clothing.

MEP: Wow! So it really is a strip club?!

Abdul X: Yes. You can actually see their whole face.

Quick, Name a Muslim Charity

Can you name a Muslim charity that provides help to people around the world? Think hard.

Most people would have no problem naming a charity that provides for people around the world, such as Red Cross, United Way, Salvation Army, Catholic Charities, Habitat for Humanity, Heart Association, UNICEF, Cancer Society—and the list goes on. But the name of a Muslim charity that does that the same work would be hard to find.

A recent article in Huffington Post claims that Muslims are the most giving people in the world according to statistics and put them ahead of Christians and Jews in charitable donations. The article, however, doesn't make distinctions between those charities that are listed as terror organizations and those that aren't.

Not separating them would be similar to counting contributions to the KKK or the Nazi party as charities in the same category as The Make A Wish Foundation. That would be an irrational thought. Many Muslim charities gave millions to Al Qaeda, Boko Haram, Hamas and other organizations worldwide as organizations that killed people instead of helping them.

Now, if you were able to think of a Muslim charity at all, you might have come up with something like Islamic Relief or Muslim Aid. However, both of these organizations have been tied to terror organizations. So, it begs the question, "Why are so many Muslim charities linked to terrorist organizations?"

For rational thinking individuals, the criteria for donating to a charity must meet certain requirements. First, a charity should ensure that most of the donated money will go to its mission and not used for its own operation. Second, a good charity should be financially transparent, which makes it trustworthy. Finally, a charity should not fund terror.

Let's look at just one Muslim organization operating in the U.S. and considered by some as a real charity. If you came up with C.A.I.R. (Council on American-Islamic Relations), you might think you've found one. That's a good charity, right?

WRONG!

CAIR is one of more than 80 groups around the world designated as a **terrorist organization** by the United Arab Emirates, placing it in the company of Al Qaeda, Islamic State and others. Although it is not yet listed as such in the U.S., you may have some legitimate questions about it.
☐
CAIR was created by the Muslim Brotherhood, which has been condemned by the government of Egypt. The Muslim Brotherhood is condemned because it has a history of Islamic terrorism and has sanctioned violence against its civilians.

CAIR has only about 5,000 members, despite the fact that a membership only costs $10. That's why CAIR receives financial support from foreign powers that have also provided direct support with Al Qaeda, Hamas and other terrorists. The founders of CAIR have praised terrorists for suicide bombings on behalf of Islam.

In addition, CAIR board members have called for the overthrow of the United States and the imposition of Islamic law. They have suggested Sharia law punishment (death) for people who criticize Islam or their prophet Muhammad on the internet.

While CAIR has not yet been listed as a terror organization in the U.S., more than a dozen high-level CAIR members have been under investigation for ties to Islamic terror organizations. That may be why CAIR has discouraged Muslim Americans from cooperating with law enforcement, and spend money on behalf of convicted terrorists and not for victims.

The next time you hear someone suggesting that CAIR is a charitable organization, ask the following questions.

Why does CAIR refuse to condemn the killing of Americans in uniform? Why doesn't CAIR condemn Hamas? Does CAIR really want to see Islamic law as the law of the land in America? Why has CAIR refused to condemn the Islamic Republic of Sudan for the deaths of 200,000 Christian Africans in the name of jihad? Does CAIR believe in equal rights for all religions?

The quest continues for the name of a legitimate Muslim charity that provides help for people worldwide regardless of their religious affiliation. Don't hold your breath.

Hitler/Mohammad's Time Warp

Imagine yourself back in time, just a little over 70 years ago. Imagine it is the spring of 1943 and the war against fascism is being fought on two fronts—Europe and the Pacific. The war in Europe against Hitler and his Nazis are still a real threat, but imagine that news comes that Hitler has been killed by a special ops team that infiltrated Hitler's bunker and killed him.

The news report that this special ops team collected all the maps, letters, plans and related information about Nazi spies, operations and intelligence in Germany, England, America and throughout the world. Included in the raid are thousands of pieces of information that would give the Allies a decided edge in stopping the war and saving many lives.

Imagine that FDR, the American president, announced that Hitler is dead and the Nazis are "on the run." As a result of that announcement, FDR tells his intelligence personnel that there is no urgency to analyze all the information gathered by the special ops team.

Furthermore, FDR decides to take most of his intelligence analysts away from deciphering all the information gathered from the bunker, and he spends the next few years (while the war continues) giving his attention to a new scientific report alleging that the world truly is flat after all.

Yes, I know. That's all imaginary, right? We all know that Hitler killed himself (or was assassinated as some say) when he saw the war was going against him and he couldn't win. While the Allies did discover some information (maps, letters, plans, etc. at various times during WWII) that helped shorten the war, but in the end, the Allies won the war against Hitler and his fascists.

There was no special ops team that killed Hitler. FDR did not announce that the Nazis were "on the run" and he did not reassign his intelligence specialists to other ridiculous news. The war did end and America, Europe and the world was saved from the hell planned by Hitler. This scenario is just imaginary.

But we are in a time warp!

Recently a report in *The Weekly Standard*, detailed that the May 2011 raid on Osama bin Laden's Pakistani compound yielded more than one million documents, including DVDs, ten hard drives, a dozen cell phones, and almost 100 thumb drives (flash drives). It is called "the single largest collection of senior terrorist materials ever."

However, Colonel Derek Harvey, says the intelligence community has analyzed less than 10 percent of the collection. According to officials, they were told directly to stop providing analyses based on the bin Laden documents. That's incredible! In addition, Obama says the biggest threat to the world is from global warming. Why is the POTUS closing his mind to finding more info from the material gathered when Osama bin Laden was killed?

Because it refuted Obama's boast that al-Qaeda was "on the run."

"The administration had decided to end the war on terror, and no amount of new intelligence about threats from al Qaeda was going to change their minds," according to Stephen Hayes in The Weekly Standards's report. "So they chose ignorance."

Is this Nobel Peace Prize winner trying to deflect FACTS away from the truth that fundamental Islam is not a religion of peace as he and many others claim? Is our POTUS a traitor to America and our Allies?

Don't Be Fooled! Islam ≠ Peace

Liberals lie. And much of their lies protect the murderous intentions of Islamic terrorists.

When they don't outright lie, they slant the truth in such a way that, when closely investigated, even young children can see through their lies.

Recently, I read an article by a liberal publication that claimed that the majority of terror attacks (in the U.S. and worldwide) were not conducted by Muslims or people with Islamic intentions. Several claims in the article were outrageous. Here's one example:

"In fact in 2013, it was actually more likely Americans would be killed by a toddler than a terrorist. In that year, three Americans were killed in the Boston Marathon bombing. How many people did toddlers kill in 2013? Five, all by accidentally shooting a gun." (*The Daily Beast*)

Why did the recent article refer to 2013 when more recent years are available (2014, for example)? Like all years of terrorist activity, statistics have their ups and downs and 2013 is one of those years. Last year was not chosen since it wouldn't prove their point. I've included the details of 2014 and the first 3 months of 2015 at the end of this article, which disproves their theory.

While it is true that only 3 people actually died from that attack, the Beast ignores the FACT that more than 200 others were injured and 16 actually lost limbs from the attack, including a 7-year-old girl. This attack was conducted by two Muslim brothers, one of which is currently on trial for the attack. My search for details produced that no infants playing with guns resulted in anyone losing a limb or hundreds of others being injured by the accidents.

Intentional half-truths

The intentionally misleading article in the *Beast* continued to present half-truths.

"Honestly, when is the last time we heard the media refer to those who attack abortion clinics as "Christian terrorists," even though these attacks occur at one of every five reproductive health-care facilities? That doesn't sell as well. After all we are a so-called Christian nation, so that would require us to look at the enemy within our country, and that makes many uncomfortable. Or worse, it makes them change the channel."

Honestly?

While attacks on abortion clinics (places where people go to murder helpless children--let's call it by its real name and not the whitewashed name of "reproductive health-care facilities") were more common in the 1990s, only one person has been murdered by an anti-abortion activist since 2000. No attempted murders, assaults and/or kidnapping are recorded since 1998. In fact, attacks on abortion clinics since 2000 (using 15 years of statistics) have amounted only to 13 attempts of arson, bombing and property damage since 2000.

My investigation of these attacks show that these so-called "attacks" by the *Beast* resulted in no injuries and only property damage. That means that no person was beheaded, hung, pushed from a building, buried alive or locked in a cage and burned alive. Readers of the *Daily Beast* may want to take notes of these facts in case they find themselves on the TV show "Are You Smarter Than a 5th Grader?"

The liberal article continues by warning readers to beware of conservative media "discussing how we can we stop these scary brown Muslims from killing any more Americans despite the fact you actually have a better chance of being killed by a refrigerator falling on you." The statistics they are referring to ones produced from agencies like the U.S. Consumer Product Safety Commission.

While it is true that a number of people are UNINTENTIONALLY killed when televisions, furniture and refrigerators are killed each year, it must be remembered that they are accidents and not planned by a terrorist person or group. The are called accidents because, in nearly every case, precautions could have prevented the death.

The *Beast* concludes the article by trying to make readers embarrassed by ridiculous fears of Islamic terrorism. It does this by saying, "I'm not saying to ignore the dangers posed by Islamic radicals. I'm just saying look out for those refrigerators."

The *Beast* would have Americans forget September 11, 2001 when thousands of Americans died from Islamic terrorists and be more concerned that your flat screen TV is properly attached to your living room wall. These articles are the ones that liberals think are cute, but discount real attacks and attempts being conducted on a daily basis by Muslims here and around the world.

As promised, here are the number of Muslim terror attacks in 2014 that resulted in deaths as recorded by Wikipedia. It is important to note that this is NOT the total number of attacks by Muslims, but only the number that resulted in deaths.

Number of Muslim terror attacks (with deaths) in 2014

January 1, 2014 – Killed Palestinian ambassador "held explosive in his hands". 1 dead terrorist.[37][38] /wiki/Nigeria/wiki/Nigeria

February 14, 2014 – Borneo Massacre at least 200 killed by Boko Haram[39] /wiki/China/wiki/China

March 1, 2014 – A group of 8 individuals attacked civilians at Kunming Railway Station, 28 dead, 143 wounded. /wiki/China/wiki/China

April 30, 2014 – Two assailants attacked passengers and detonated explosives at the Ürümqi railway station, 3 dead, 79 wounded. /wiki/Nigeria/wiki/Nigeria

May 20, 2014 – Jos bombings at least 118 killed and over 56 injured[40] /wiki/China/wiki/China

May 22, 2014 – Two SUVs which carried 5 assailants were driven into a street market in Ürümqi and up to a dozen explosives were thrown at shoppers through the windows of the SUVs. The cars then crashed into shoppers and collided into each other and exploded, 39 dead, 90+ wounded. /wiki/Belgium/wiki/Belgium

May 24, 2014 – Jewish Museum of Belgium shooting. Gunman opened fire at the Jewish Museum in Brussels killing 4 people. /wiki/Syria/wiki/Syria

August 2014 – Islamic State fighters massacred some 700 people, mostly men, of the Shu'aytat tribe in Deir ez-Zor Governorate.[41] /wiki/Australia/wiki/Australia

September 23, 2014 – 2014 Endeavour Hills stabbings. Numan Haider, an Afghan Australian stabbed two counter terrorism officers in Melbourne, Australia. He was then shot dead.[42] /wiki/Russia/wiki/Russia

October 5, 2014 – 2014 Grozny bombing. 5 officers and the suicide bomber, were killed, while 12 others were wounded.[43] /wiki/Canada/wiki/Canada

October 20, 2014 – 2014 Saint-Jean-sur-Richelieu ramming attack. Lone attacker used his car to run over two Canadian soldiers. 1 killed, 1 injured /wiki/Canada/wiki/Canada

October 22, 2014 – 2014 shootings at Parliament Hill, Ottawa. Lone attacker shot a soldier at a war memorial and attacked

Parliament. 1 killed, 3 injured.[44]
/wiki/United_States/wiki/United_States

October 23, 2014 – Zale H. Thomson, also known as Zaim
Farouq Abdul-Malik, attacked four New York policemen in the
subway with a hatchet, severely injuring one in the back of the
head and injuring another policeman in the arm before being shot
to death by the remaining officers, who also shot a bystander.[45]
/wiki/Nigeria/wiki/Nigeria

November 28, 2014 – Kano bombing. Around 120 people were
killed and another 260 injured.[46][47][48][49]
/wiki/United_Arab_Emirates/wiki/United_Arab_Emirates

December 1, 2014 – A burqa-clad woman stabs a 47-year-old
American teacher to death in a mall restroom in Abu Dhabi. She
later plants a bomb outside the home of an Egyptian-American
doctor, which was safely dismantled.[50]
/wiki/Russia/wiki/Russia

December 4, 2014 – 2014 Grozny clashes. 26 total dead,
including 14 policemen, 11 Jihadist from Caucasus Emirate, 1
civilian[51] /wiki/Australia/wiki/Australia

December 15, 2014 – 2014 Sydney hostage crisis. 2 dead, 4
injured.[52][53][54][55][56][57][58][59][60]
/wiki/Pakistan/wiki/Pakistan

December 16, 2014 – 2014 Peshawar school attack. Over 140
people dead, including at least 132 children.[61]
/wiki/Yemen/wiki/Yemen

December 16, 2014 – Two suicide car bombers rammed their
vehicles into a Shiite rebels' checkpoint killing 26, including 16
students.[62] /wiki/Nigeria/wiki/Nigeria

December 18, 2014 – 2014 Gumsuri kidnappings. Boko Haram
insurgents killed 32 men and kidnapped at least 185 women and
children.[63] /wiki/Syria/wiki/Syria

December 18, 2014 – Mass grave of 230 Tribesmen killed by Islamic State found in Eastern Syria.[64]
/wiki/France/wiki/France

December 20, 2014 – 2014 Joué-lès-Tours stabbings. A man yelling Allahu Akbar attacked a police office with a knife. He was killed and 3 police officers were injured
/wiki/France/wiki/France

December 21, 2014 – 2014 Dijon attack. A man yelling Allahu Akbar ran over 11 pedestrians with his vehicle. 11 injured
/wiki/Nigeria/wiki/Nigeria

December 22, 2014 – Boko Haram insurgents bombed a bus station in the city of Gombe, killing at least twenty people.[65]
/wiki/Iraq/wiki/Iraq

December 2014 – Islamic State militants execute 150 women Iraqi province of Al-Anbar, some of whom were pregnant at the time, who refuse to marry their fighters.[66] /wiki/Iraq/wiki/Iraq

December 24, 2014 – A suicide bomber killed 33 people and wounded 55 others in Madaen, about 25 km (15 miles) south of Baghdad.[67] /wiki/Somalia/wiki/Somalia

December 25, 2014 – Al-Shabaab attack in Mogadishu leaves 9 dead.[68] /wiki/Cameroon/wiki/Cameroon

December 28, 2014 – Boko Haram attacks village in Cameroon leaving 30 dead.[69]

The number of people killed in 2014 by Muslims in terror attacks stands at 1,925 with more than 700 occurring in December (only 4 months ago). This does not include the thousands upon thousands of injuries, loss of limbs, rapes and kidnappings during the same period.

Don't let any liberals publications or media fool you. Muslims terror attacks are on the rise. From January 2015 until the present (April 7, 2015), more than 600 people have been killed by Muslims who follow the teachings of Muhammad (the false prophet of Islam).

Number of Muslim terror attacks with deaths in 2015 (so far)

January 7–9, 2015 – A series of 5 attacks in and around Paris kill 17 people, plus 3 attackers, and leave 22 other people injured. /wiki/Nigeria/wiki/Nigeria

January 8, 2015 – 2015 Baga massacre. Boko Haram attacks town of Baga in northern Nigeria killing at least 200 people. Another 2000 are unaccounted for.[70] /wiki/Pakistan/wiki/Pakistan

January 30, 2015 – Suicide bomber kills at least 55, injuring at least 59 in a Shiite mosque in southern Pakistan.[71] /wiki/Pakistan/wiki/Pakistan

February 13, 2015 – Heavily armed militants killed at least 19 people and wounded more than 40 after they stormed into a Shiite mosque during Friday Prayer in a suburb of Peshawar. [72] /wiki/Denmark/wiki/Denmark

February 14–15, 2015 – 2015 Copenhagen attacks. A gunman opened fire at the Krudttoenden café and later at the Great Synagogue in Copenhagen, killing two civilians and injuring five others.[73] /wiki/Pakistan/wiki/Pakistan

March 15, 2015 – Suicide bombers kill at least 15 people in attacks on two churches in Lahore.[74] /wiki/Tunisia/wiki/Tunisia

March 18, 2015 – Bardo National Museum attack. Militants linked to Islamic State attack the Bardo National Museum with guns, killing 21 people and injuring around 50.[75]

/wiki/Yemen/wiki/Yemen

March 20, 2015 – 2015 Sana'a mosque bombings. 135 killed in bombings on several mosques by Islamic State.[76]
/wiki/Kenya/wiki/Kenya

April 2, 2015 – 148 killed in Al-Shabaab's Garissa University College attack.[77]

Don't let liberals or Muslims (who continue to profess that Islam is a religion of peace) fool you. The religion of Muhammad is **<u>NOT</u>** peaceful at all.

Muslims: We Can't Control Ourselves

Can behavior of many Muslims be called abnormal behavior? Is their behavior due to psychological problems they are unable to control?

Here's how most psychologists describe this behavior:

"Many psychological problems are characterized by a loss of control or a lack of control in specific situations. Usually, this lack of control is part of a pattern of behavior that also involves other maladaptive thoughts and actions." (Psychology Information Online)

This loss of control is usually accompanied by other problems including sexual disorders such as pedophilia.

"When loss of control is only a component of a disorder, it usually does not have to be a part of the behavior pattern, and other symptoms must also be present for the diagnosis to be made."

Some of these other psychological disorders (accentuated by loss of control) include Internittent Explosive Disorder, Domestic Violence, Kleptomania, Pyromania and Pedophilia, as already mentioned.

Five Reasons Why Islam May Result in a Mental Disorder

1.) According to psychologists, **Intermittent Explosive Disorder** is described as "episodes of aggressive outbursts resulting in either destruction of property or physical assaults on others. Typically, this problem results in legal problems as well."

Psychologists say that the individual exhibiting this behavior is usually a male who has had several other incidents of losing control of anger and the result is either by assaulting others, or destroying property.

For months, reasonable people have attempted to find out why jihadists and members of the Islamic State are so angry. Last month I published an article entitled "8 Anger Management Tips for Moderate Muslims" and it is hoped that followers of Mohammad will put these tips into practice and help them adapt to citizens of the 21st century.

Now it is hoped that my readers will begin to understand that radical Muslims are actually "acting out" behaviors that are part of their ideology. Even Louis Farrakhan, leader of many black American Muslims, said recently that "there is no moderate Islam."

2.) Explosive Domestic Violence (EDV) is described as a particular form of Intermittent Explosive Disorder. With EDV, it is exhibited in the context of a close interpersonal relationship. When this behavior is accompanied with alcohol, it is usually attributed to the consumption of alcohol.

However, in cases where alcohol is not involved, it is labeled as EDV. In cases of EDV involving alcohol, intoxication is another way of not accepting blame for the behavior. In extreme cases of EDV, the blame is always the fault of the victim.

In the cases of Muslim men raping their wives, Muslim men find the fault in the wife. In cases of raping women not their wives, the blame is also with the victim for wearing garments or items that entice or lure a man to act out and rape them.

3.) Kleptomania is another problem stemming from lack of control. This is a rare disorder in most societies. In some societies, however, it is ingrained in their ideology and justified by directing the activity only toward those not a particular segment of society.

In the case of Islam, piracy (stealing from infidels and others) has been part of their society for more than a century. Following the American Revolution, the first war engaged by Americans were against Muslims (Barbary Pirates) who were stealing from U.S. merchants, including kidnapping and holding them for ransom.

4.) Pyromania is a psychological problem that many people recognize as a mania of "setting fires for pleasure, and experiencing a sense of relief or gratification from the experience." This is separate from setting fires for monetary gain or to hide criminal activity.

Some psychologists believe that it does not include behavior that expresses anger. However, with the advent of ISIS and behavior that includes setting people on fire in cages may require psychologists to re-examine the behavior and classify this type of abnormal behavior as another example of an anger disorder.

5.) Pedophilia is a disorder that manifests in which adults have intense and recurrent sexual urges about prepubescent children, usually 13 years old and younger. In the case of Muslim men, again there is a long history of pedophilia. Many use the example of their prophet Mohammad as an excuse for their abnormal behavior. In fact, in Islam he is called the perfect man.

In Summary

To sum it all up, all five of these mental disorders are evident and prevalent in Islam. While some of these disorders are seen in individuals within all societies, it is widespread in Islam to such a degree that it is difficult to diagnose a cure.

As with all diseases or mental disorders, there may be only two possible solutions. One is surgery and the other is radiation. Society may have to decide which is the best solution.

2015 ISIS Mujahideen Calendar

Jihadists are determined not to be left behind in any area of life, and the Islamic State's 2015 Mujahideen Calendar is living proof.

Although we are already into April, I was able to trade a year's supply of chickpeas and garlic for the 2015 ISIS Calendar with . . . you guessed it, a bevy of beautiful camels. With no further introductions, here's the coveted calendar.

MISS JANUARY
When winter winds blow across the Mongolian Desert, who wouldn't want to cuddle up with Miss January? This Asian bactrian beauty prefers free ranging areas and loves alfalfa and oats.

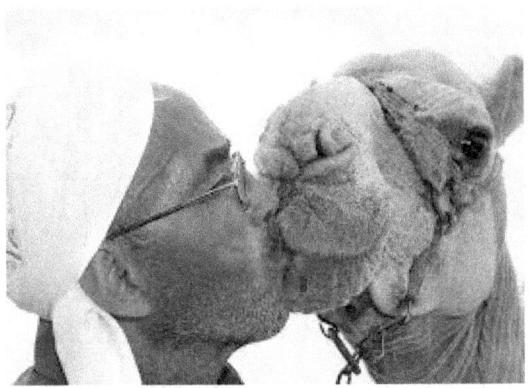

MISS FEBRUARY

As Valentine's Day draws near, love is obviously in the air. But it would be easy to fall in love with Miss February. She's a terrorist's dream come true, especially when jihadi brides are hard to come by.

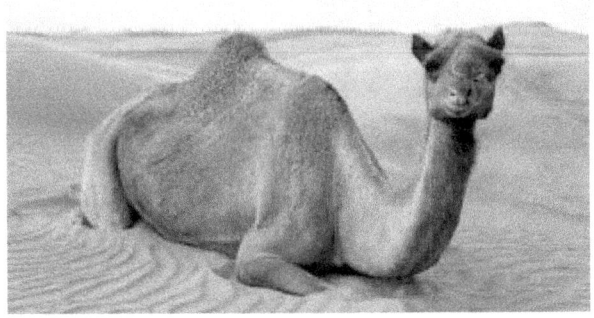

MISS MARCH

Classical lines and the curvature of her neck make Miss March every Arab jealous of her owner. This dromedary loves soaking up the sun and long walks in the desert.

MISS APRIL
No fool would ignore this high stepping beauty. She was
unanimously selected as Miss April. She likes to perform almost
any time of the day or night.

MISS MAY
Miss May is of noble birth and likes to be adorned with bangles
and beads. She may appear to be all show, but looks can be
deceiving.

MISS JUNE
What's more fun to watch than a wet camel contest? Miss June is guaranteed to bring hours of fun into the life of any mujahid and break up the time when there no infidels are in sight.

MISS JULY
Who respectable terrorist wouldn't want to take a tumble in the hay with Miss July? A real down-to-earth dromedary, she likes hay of course, as well as dates and olives.

MISS AUGUST

Double your pleasure, double your fun. We couldn't choose which of these albino twins should grace the page of the calendar for Miss August, so we chose both of them.

MISS SEPTEMBER

Ready to be mounted and carry you into the thick of the battle, Miss September will not let you down until you're ready to dismount. When jihadi brides are not available, she's a faithful companion.

MISS OCTOBER
What a beauty! This bactrian from the high desert plateaus of
Mongolia is the envy of Islamic terrorist. Miss October enjoys it
when the weather changes and days get cooler.

MISS NOVEMBER
If you can't afford a jihadi bride with a burka, you'll be happy
with this young camel with her own modest garment. Miss
October can be more acceptable when you drape a hijab over her
head.

MISS DECEMBER
The year 2015 will end on a high note with Miss December. She chose a very colorful outfit that accents many of her curves and submissive manner.

www.ingramcontent.com/pod-product-compliance
Lightning Source LLC
Chambersburg PA
CBHW070838290526
45795CB00002B/906